VEXED

Jessica Grim

BlazeVOX [books]
Buffalo, New York

Vexed by Jessica Grim

Copyright © 2009

Published by BlazeVOX [books]

All rights reserved. No part of this book may be reproduced without the publisher's written permission, except for brief quotations in reviews.

Vexed was first published by /ubu Editions in 2002 as an electronic book; thanks to Brian Kim Stefans & Kenny Goldsmith

Printed in the United States of America

Book design by Geoffrey Gatza
Cover image: Lantern slide of Mohave Desert, tree, Mohave Desert, CA; Courtesy of the Frances Loeb Library, Harvard Graduate School of Design

First Print Edition

ISBN: 9781935402152
Library of Congress Control Number: 2008943145

BlazeVOX [books]
14 Tremaine Ave
Kenmore, NY 14217

Editor@blazevox.org

publisher of weird little books

BlazeVOX [books]

blazevox.org

2 4 6 8 0 9 7 5 3 1

Contents

Vapors 9

I

Fall 2001 13
Untitled 15
Seats of Mercy 16
Turf 18
Convention (1) 20
Convention (2) 21
Topography 22
Transcontinent 24
Inauguration 25
November 2000 27
The Visionary 29
America 31
Pensacola 32
San Simeon 33

II

Parable of the Valley & Days 37

III

The Wait 49
Untitled 51
House Poem No. 1 52

Pelee	55
Preterm (The Tourist)	57
Twos	60
The Symptom	62
02.02.02	66
The Youngest Pod	68
But even once you can see the fruits	70
House Poem No. 2	71

VEXED

Vapors

And that which we cannot fathom will not
gracefully

befits
adhesive image of a man on a
rock high above a valley taking a photo

what is actual   transcribed
varieties

the trace so benign

avider
up across and overhand to the accountant

behold
mid-summer grass browns it is
a verb lacking
precision

the embodied embassy
low-cal word set
          multiple multiples materialize

ennui epicenter

it appears grandiose

hominid tract
in mid sway

parochial flinch

to say or not say it the same
way

come, little onion,
this is nothing and you know it

vapors

I

Fall 2001

Hardly anyone from this life was there

day pass people
move slowly about
their business

their having been willing to die

local man makes news for painting his
house as a flag

"reality tv"

the further you stand from the
wall the further the wall has to fall
      now
the market's in trouble

sand point

beige days   we decide
our retaliation

surely the beet
with its blood sweet heart
would do   instead

a book in which a boy sails across the
sky on a lounge chair

a book in which all this happens

we are fighting to think our way clear

a plausible explanation

emotional retardant
a surrogate heart
demented honeydew

harvest fest to end all harvest fests, let
me think

        shrill wax moon the
calm depends upon

laterally there is some cause for optimism

so, let's assume another world view

"At Baghdad's Museum of Natural History a missile put a two-foot hole in a wall and shattered glass display cases for stuffed lions and hyenas."

month of the water rat
day of the metal ox
hour of the earth pig

stuttered
seeing captions as text

spatial depth obligates vision to
engagement its
sensory
ill will
notwithstanding
      a plying of the waters what
      waters
the old ones

warm war-time weather the world over

but it has the *texture* of felicity

inferring a kind of scarlet

analog meaning there's a face to it

Untitled

Peculiar appearance without
which he may very well have been mistaken
for the forest tarpaulin
blowing forward
into the zone

it is not clear to me what is at stake

in the event that one is leapt over

        a sound which rang out   thrills

approximates ample time
their
want of something
having eagerly

as in an undying love

into the warming night their
imagination   unfolded
for want of a hero for want of
a heroine
clambering to become
upright

Seats of Mercy

Relative norm capsized
all ilk turned out
imperative dalliance, the
copper cringe
a tour of your life's travails

sobriquet
tinselly
"why wait a very long time or forever?"
they've met the night for the final time

first person transparent
clinical calling
quiz ravens

the veils as worn by the pilot
        halo effect
imagine   dawn   remedy

felt-tip fingers   how convenient
        it materializes on her forehead when
sun hits her
face   having lived in the wrong era
            for that

poetics fuse
stutter
       pedant moon

inkblacknight.com
        insofar as I remember
        light thrown backwards onto
              "our own youth"
in the crib

tie actions to the person
unavoidable moderations
drip indicator

speeded up to show the actual dental work
while on the asphalt the acquired taste
totally flipped

squid licks
        fabled vertigo
the seats of mercy

Turf

       Exiting left
thought cogs
upset
burls to surface

black birds w/blue heads in the grass

crucially   thus

not any more or less preposterous

historically exhausted

the torso also
securing   the hope even if you'd never wanted it

civilians crouch
bravery saved them

"All of our population in all of their chronically ill areas."

vocables
     narrative occludes
enticing sitting stiller

a torpor-like enthusiasm

hot still town in the high plains
blows away

graduating into ever smaller units

most   agreeable   atmospheres   comply

cruel cruel real estate
organizationally   in piles

secularly cool
wind winding down

"some survived by falling and pretending to be dead"
"as they are depicted in the NATO photo"

"in the charred remains of their houses"

boy after eating leans

coal blink

as they had themselves been
wedging ponderously between the house and the cliff

heats' display
        numbered 1 to 10
        sabbatical torque tips
across   crisp

face reddens   when walked away
from

why
        start
     to hum & fuss & creak

show the delicate life you're up for it

his ducal responsibility

     see the absence of sea air here?
heady hang of those vines
thick waxy leaves
   trope announces

with what blunt instrument?
     not a strand in sight
where your writing is imaginatively glimmering

Convention (1)

Criteria for contentment
      abbreviates
memory of what my practice is

increased verve   composite sketch of
small violent burst of some kind of pod or
nut
      breaking apart

range of sound   intervals

they crave a symbol

      sky-blue underside

airlift morals

      while, above, the light
serving your plot
in the capacity of an atom
getting hotter

Convention (2)

Sharksuit tea
lily pad suite
algebra's beginning to ache

a very convincing
cumin
loaded with
        empathy

pulmonary switch

        same rhetoric capsized
              sugary sugary
        slimming tan
offsets motherhood

              zone bland haze
    now at
cruising level
weighted well above the norm

Topography

These lines drawn across the continent

dust on the freeway kicks up
        withering trance

        criteria poised to look
like   really being   something

        risk of seizure associated

willful acquisition of attitude
        may cause
        one morning I was
approached by a nun
        in my own home

deepen the dependence

just off the plane
captivate
the former boxing legend

row of houses robust in the winter dusk
        mind of a prelingual child
leaves no stain

contingent urgent

out of infancy straight into
the dog house

memories formed without words
the ointment, please

objects gather period dust
sunless light
suggestive of time

inks' spot expands on
        faux terrazzo

        a longing relates to language

always

partake of gestation
indices

regard the gaze through
partially drawn curtains

whatever you are moved
to do

is that "puncture" or "perforate"?

lose view to reflection
pragmatism's tilt

wash that
skill set slurry
      over the entire
typical
three-point sanctuary

pandemonium is
      windless

squire   quill   fusebox
fume stood still

Transcontinent

Pressure of sediment
        imagine destination as
ubiquitous
hills' top   elegized life
go away   to
        assume
other   crossbred
        parts,
a great deal   more
fine-featuredness
        scarred
peculiar compulsion to
record   fixative
trenchant
writ in dark
rabid   wakes to say
"mommy daddy"
desire for tradition
prevails
        leave space in dawn light
their brethren   the crane in the valley

Inauguration

Sequencing
pure vocal energy

torpidarium
        incumbent pouch
          tedium shores up
just a seizure short of sanity

arms out   *you* tell *me* who survived
      and how

pelted   rebate
cultivar
not a bright enough white for whom?

a credit to his stigma

irregular beam
incisors attract
      that meat
surreptitiously

the hagiographer's dream

in which hair is "pigmented filaments"

scarlet integer

what are its intentions?

cold front
seaside arabesque

sure fire inert
     fidelity

clinging to its heart
the small animal made its way across the road

sheer off just below the thought line

a shelf upon which to put it

       out of its misery

intercept best wish flurry
       emblem festers

fragments of morality float by

they are catching their breath or would
you have called it a "revisit"

narrative miff –
the more end in sight the better

lethal logic
coefficient
grimace

misgivings kindle incident
spring rains
scorch at
syllable-level
enter it here:
       famous grid chart

becoming their own dream of themselves

November 2000

Days pass
hope deteriorates

are they demotable?

only the skidmarks on your face

which calls on itself for support

no satisfiable
        whim
could be identified
        long blowing grasses &
leaf piles
        domesticate the national depression

exactly which nondescript do you mean?

there's a lot of the vernacular in that tableaux

first light flurries

all tuckered out by the inquiry

carcinogen cocktail
true blue anxiety
pendulum

several fixed emotive states

fanning reassurance

the designee assigns himself

wildflowers' seed pod up over the snow
line feeds birds

winterize your dismay

        a wink like an
indentation   in the ceiling —
it brings its meaning up close to itself but

delivers nothing

you can almost see a personality emerging

The Visionary

Epiphany   truncated
searing exhaustion

ecstatic tomb

frankly, item #2: the gauntlet:
      starting at the elbow the sleeve
            hovering slightly
technical weaves
      bladed score
      upsetable,
            humming in the ego barn
the grange the eye-color lives on
(still episodic)

verisimilitude   touts,
      overly subjective opinion
rudders
      by the book
        opposite of slaved,
            piquant

      as per the ounce
            able to will the thought

composite of farce
& desire
      branches barely
        sway in reflection patterning
cumulative   expenditure of energies   evenly

since you're going that way

a siltier tense than
present

charming saturate
so many blanks stop
& watch the brain develop
awhile
      filling
up the environment as the environment

wants
        the teariness

in the pit

the astronauts could barely
walk, what history?

phenomena

        windows fanned with ice

as crude as the next
optimist

crate up antibodies

regarding the tense lack of imagination

water with an expiration date

reasoning crease
ticking off on fingers

which in fact means the earth's lower
atmosphere hasn't warmed measurably

America

Dusked
avalanche a conviction
for the dragging
death   having been disturbed
        pre-spring
coagulant
variations of "cooped up"
as surely
as that sunlight
        a civilian   among you
hibernating
entranced
colossal   excuse
        for that

"The butterfly reserves have
never been popular with the local people"

Dear Them,
my arm was twisted
around my head   since
passing the fan in the other
room
        turns

Pensacola

For security reasons
airborne enzyme
       creased pelican pelt
making a mockery of the middle distance
tungsten   creel
beta version
toward that end it's
karaoke day
at the zoo

pink light in the east whitens
through the blinds

each deceit
tundra
on a cliff a man
writes a note

San Simeon
for Laura Moriarty

Solitary   engagement
dust sways in the grid
all quest   suspense

The forward one leans as if to catch herself   there
making space negative   notorious
light breaking through

Splice mood with facts, temperature,
hours   the concave road
alabaster, categorical

Scale of the illusion, silken epithets
black lines above the perimeter
negate where the sound still rang out

Apparition reappears
the past by its own sequence
is ornate, vehicular

The distance seeming to
hinder possibility   a peculiar
western stillness

II

Parable of the Valley & Days
[Woodside Calif., May 1997]

Sloughing off precedent days

anticipate sounds at night
the solitary calm original
hill   twinged   swept across the sky

they have no way to know what they will be like in the open

•

    Cleave from social   a little human sound
toppling

cold wind now

lingers

•

If you can sit
quietly enough
    not even a breeze to
disturb

    eager
walk
species-specific

the never-ending nearness
to the end

•

Brightens hills in streaks the green
there   stops
in or out of
accord

cautiously   growing   lawns

•

Text upsets limbs' lightheaded habits

it is crucial   phantomlike   we could be anywhere —

saturation of mid-day sun soaking into color

phobic integer   amplifies surrounding
      surround —

the catapult within
      — potentate

•

Carries over the valley's gears

you might find it useful to have with you a guide to the region

entropy balloons   —   out over the
      order —
cohabitate deck   park   garden allows the mounds to grow

wishing for a fragrance more than an actual place —

      the heat too much — butane —

escape is theoretical
blue cornflowers

speaking of an historical moment as if this were an historical moment

alchemical hip

      reflectivity

wait to evoke   slippage

carefully   perched
   by the same token scarcely
perceivable
the bulk   obdurately   & the grasses

          epoch tilt
          scrubbing up

> *the continuous*
> *present just got*
> *past*
>
> *do not keep saying "the hills" do not*
> *keep saying "green" do not keep*
> *saying "sky", above all*
>
> *raving example*
>
> *perhaps the music would be less harmful if we swallowed it first,*
>   *then took the pills*
>
> *stump painting*

•

The mountain carp are swimming
away

curled plum
as in the heavy flower head
    bends

      measure   restlessness

in the valley the mere mention

parallel flanks   swept up

•

    You keep calling
home the fantasy

flurries like you've never seen

counteract
   the page   the
  sun   pumps

having forgotten about
    whatever
     stance

    those are animals
who move   slowly
           if
                    at all

remember me   to them

         brightening acres   fluid on the
         behavior   brazen

         holding the world to your head

         sped downhill how do you
         contextualize it?

•

    Between the
plan & your heart

acre-sized   figure of speech
    pale

in the labyrinths'
    entry

they fell from it

        the bushes are actually white, along the fence which is actually white.
        and in the white white sky, the most white of all

•

There is a peacefulness a terror
    out there for the
balancing

squinting at the spot where the sky meets the hilltop

the several inmates became
my pretend adornment

(atonal)

think   tank   plunge

      empty arenas   sequential   not until it's nearly over   the city enters
      the mind in absence

      excuse lassitude

      the oppositional ego
      feels free to expand

      (patriarch tips
      his hat)

      the epitome of another flower grew, in the corner

•

Voluptuary
delicate
at the
    turning point —
    schematic

      show us the real me

      the tiny hummingbirds

      I imagine the landscape to've sparkled then   crisp
      outlines & colors in the early morning nothing having yet succumbed
      to the heat

      bravely   tumbling
      what the wish was   in the trees

      implosion is what you make of it

•

You choose your heroes they do not occur
naturally   inside the vase

each day
the cool
    early eve

green green gray

dome

porous
voices carry

       jet appears to make no headway
       cultivate
       courageous aim   (yet the aim itself raises
       no welt)

•

There must be an
alternate reality we could all
subscribe to —

your turn to
    try   being able to see

twice as much of you as you seem
willing to give

the knee alone

we cannot recognize you for who you
say you are is that our
problem or yours?

•

Breeze this a.m. from the
north, or northeast
     subcutaneous lunge   grovel—

reticulate
bench

spinose

(no I here)

brilliant white cumulous

the ship enhances the shore
pulsating horizontally

•

Please
leave the stems for the others the
weather   floated across us
    then

rustlings   emote
    feeling
grave   the stand the
     clue
melodrama

they move toward the ceremony with
     fissures closing around them

when will this be possible? —

then they line up for feeding

linear
of or near floating

        the landscape was very cunning it was very fitful

•

Some years later

yellow layer of toxins above the sea
nets hold up the

   coloration

        every day you wish for

•

Nothing wants a road to itself more

    reserved for the shape of a human hand   alone
the same having been said of
the creature garden, blooming

    cartographical contusion

    outside all over the continent bands of life are tightening

•

Holes in the amber dawn   cave
in on sleep   berry stain, the slow moving
heart
    if you will notice for a moment

families lived there too they
    had to

•

    Peculiar
howling commences

        wide plank
    boats
    look less angelic by
day

the figurative sphinx

cooler water   colors lemon

I have always loved whatever it is I have
said I have always loved —

source   text
    half the time you do

•

    The leisure of your assurance your
    steadfastness

smooth mold of the Aegean
    — a feeling a
vacuum
    made from the same material

    we want
less brutality generally
    on our hillsides

proving once again
that the sentence never ends

·

Brilliant   day

radiance befitting
the lunatic month

underside   fledgling
    breathing normally—
upturned   on the current

it is not the specificity
      in *sync*   orbit

we cannot prove we were there

    interstitial
    polarity-ridden
luminary

·

Fragile as in   "the fragile plural"

the glade in the mind
      breaks just perceptibly —

softening in the rain
receiving communications
      but it fades and seems to evaporate as
the situation on the mtn. becomes
    more   *dire* —

pay attention to the burning sensation

— land appears to tip here
against this rug

you have all the information you need

reprieve

    thickening, translucent

and in the end what is the end quietly

       steely blue eyes cast
       at the door

       hills' slope

       the apogee frets

       grainy day

       the saint the fascist the servant the polite nearness in time
       of the two

       attention floats   secure
       it for me

       there is pleasure in the absence of a horde of particular recollections

•

Rustle of grasses in the wind the
    wind itself

       outer limit of desirability

       the
       root tooth

       blending into the choke grass, the skiff

       a word moored against the earth

III

The Wait

Crosses mark the eyes or sockets

snow flies horizontally or even
up
        regardless of its pitted
certitude
the realm you walk in

drifts   slow as play   photo of the stone

and what angle would that be
        forming blankets even
under the denser groups of trees

        wholly as bright
   or steady   (in some sense accurate)
they had created a meaning
out of it despite themselves

black streaks in green stone fissuring
possibly even *before* sleep

        uterine inertia

attraction of a line such as it was always falling

        extraneous   hibernation
fretful

these wks the
        shifting weight

the harsher the language the more
empty it seemed then
        cauterized
giving no clue as to content

seeing an orange glow pushed
closer to the edge

sugary hours' stride

discomfiture   quips
  spacing out to fill
space   intra
   days follow the blue moon

what's held
  to it

these things are normal
these things
are not

provisionally

slope into lack of timeline
(more likely it is more likely)
there, shadow of the pen point

resume suitability

the closer they come to the finish   to finishing
     the ornaments' claim

Untitled

Who recovers first from
an encounter with
      a word
      dream deposits another layer or
lifts it   of memory

which telling did you believe?
say "I"
      the encrusted

in the pre-existing family unit
the mother at
odds

evident

high gray sky abuts
    it   no
           sound of that
ulteriorly
      a few leaves cling

less & less   so

House Poem No. 1

Seamless   hands   alternate
resemblance

insinuated home occupies the place where the
real home stands

•

regular rooms   do

•

gracious   contour

porch   gloom   breaks
    in upon

•

ornament's organ

          to match

overly
assumed

          morning
       branches
                matters
meanwhile

sparser than ever

•

slowly toward them

   a voice
whether or not it is
          epidemic

•

in completing   truant greens

they saw a lovely light in the eye

       first lingering   intersection
shifty   notion of peace

sorry to hear the
epicenter is off
    filigree
       contagious

to tell the truth, yes.
  a crayon-like consistency
actually

•

   contralto   sweeps across blurred window
pane   in quiet heaves

   the metal breaks off
from the head
   saving them from abjection   a word
aware that in the break
      between them

•

The boy, while he's imagining this, eyes the fluid trunks of the 2 large elms. Might they even attempt to swim home?

•

sympathizing
insomniac sands

   wending your way into the foreground

acreage   ogles

to gain an even damp
    on the mix

•

     principally   starlings on the grass

  sills

        instructions to decant

.

a
surface   bloom

turning
    the less grotesque   against the
lean sky

guarded show of affection

in soft light the morning
        proves

quivered air

shall they
    observing the sun rise
            akimbo

the curvature of the earth

Pelee

Air oppressive the
whole   dottered weld   young
      child in orange cap
brightens

the word pared down into its
constituent notes

selfsame breeze males
asleep—which reminds them of a
dream they had: day two

plausible resolve

yellow
truck speeds west on
East West Road

proclaims itself
      identical that
parching

tree's leaves curl in
dry heat   this
      island dealing out an
unconsidered darkness

in so far as
night   fell

a moment
is all effect

lake snakes
for the sound of it

half-dark in which a soul has
traveled
patience beams
up at us the corollary to   seemly
in which one's dreams are of walking in a
hotter   dryer   more foreign place than

this

camphor

Preterm (The Tourist)
October—December 1998

Borrowing time or some other romance
as told by the sailors

hangs from the tree
of each night

•

Rung through haze
blighted
having gone by the wayside
the
firelight you imagined a
kind of affectation
though more durable

at the heart of the
city
giving rise to
what thought
utterant

inhabitation's
muscular pull

      palest particle
foreign —

•

Fissure flickers
in the dim light

phrases   tending to gather
on the corner
where the airwaves crackle

"profane tapestry"
certainty quivers

objects that please

•

Child in the womb moves
a corresponding ache begins to pull
at these muscles

fingers begin to articulate

       just as the water
       buoys you

which when
encountered   chills

tongue on white porcelain

•

Jagged shrubs net yellow leaves
in   wakefulness
taut by tradition
namelessness of a thing

touch billowing shirt to confirm

concierge   or   no

had they wanted to
"meaningfully" mean to

evidencing attitudes of narrative pull

culture stocks the innocent tourist

distant woods' smoke
has a tranquilizing effect on the wildlife

•

The tourist stumbles
in the early morning light

an echo
against
thinning walls

your idea of the clarity of the air   clouds

scrape them into spirals
hollowed out along the tree line

•

Shortness of breath   impinges

turning
a years' worth of participles
into that one delicate hoof

•

Gliding north a
pregnant slouch
nostalgia
"the rear of the train is behind you"

the innocent tourist coughs

and awaits
the uncertain paradigm of the offspring

Twos

To the contrary   belated
as in never

only the anointed
                    troposphere
chatting to himself

dawn   tonsure,
          Potomac
            tints of pragmatism

suitable tense flanks a moment

inseparable

a crease, a flowering tree, a crenellated fan

tyranny
gumption
boy in his room swoons

the slow unfolding of the drastic stone

a welt a rent in the tentative bond

aromatic sentence
though you may not experience it that way

whether one is flickering or fleeting

what the cause of not seeing was

infest
        complicity   coneflowers flaunt
        verdant huts
        the mention of a prevalent
        variant species

also rarely
less the machines only the birds' sounds intervene

"it is believed to be the most delicate visit of his papacy"

in which
individual blossom petals thrown into the air
hasten

a well-deserved delirium
            an
impact   a
dream lays heavily upon the table it
is a dream without urgency

the tendency

eyes just resting

in case the past turns up
missing

lone bell chime
proportionate to the tense

"prevention of feeding struggles"

borderline lingual

stratagem
provokes apathy
sparse   solvent emblem
creeping

the toddler years are upon us

The Symptom

    A bit of sun breaks
onto
collective blue
silvery   output

        up against the radiator
whom you
        timid nation foundling
    "place sulks"

that's quite some hand

  leave   them
     aside in the greenery
   in the   marvelous frame
of   late afternoon

newness   reprehensible

      life   *turned out*
   at the canopy line

a net   over the face to
  catch   or
      keep in
spring flurry of seed the
sky white
     obscures
localized
  racemes

new growth   on   evergreen's a
lighter green

plot   divines   a sentence
   overtly
      supine

supposing
for the record
 tube *cake*

    sway   against   new   shoots

humid or alphabetical?
breach or orb?

the drone and
plummet

so far, symptom-free
on some little pier all by
herself

  typical
written passage   as examined

heavy heavy heavy   lamb
    will
bear normal traffic starting tomorrow

readiness to dispense
the covered walks
the ravine
the lush hues of summer wilting
the damp cool stone a hush
a languid desire opens windows
the air still— plucking at
the garment
the overworked endive —
     focusing upon
the rose the
inspiration repository

have we missed something?

there is a certain
     incantatory molting going
on

aural thrill
lapsing

    scope & *tinge* of the cloud mass
        sanitized
just give us an easement
    calibration

ermine oddity
the surface city
an upwardness
        which
holds onto the ground
after the fingers have left it
as surely as   the observance

the
empty turn it takes   along the surface

in wartime
cluelessness
wafting on the breeze

the self
        developing another self
pelting
the softened red of the walls

into the open reality
a peculiar poverty of thought
     hunting season yet?

terminal specific to fetus
exquisitely   one form of counting
drops away
unfurling w/in the concentric splay of months leaves
     disengage in the warm humid air

           the shore would indicate
by its absence
a plan a
night with no thought of it

     the unintentional study
performs its own landscape

     the more closely it is watched the
more closely it adheres to the expectations
of the watcher
     (this is more or less true)

but w/out the taint of expectation

        pale blue — subtraction of blue
from blue what scale
it achieves

02.02.02

Every time place
thought leaves off here –

populations commence they
always   do

of the placement of things

date of birth date and city of death
all that's all that simple
really   material

smell of wax why
wax   not
entirely not
entirely the emotion

I am
ready for this to be
a vision of anyone
now

dear little one dear
son
what tethering
this
could take off
so easily weighted
only by my tenuous
hopes for
you for
humans generally the silly
hope for less   harm done

listen
even
the light breeze
there   listen — nothing
not   even
stillness

where her mind went

outside of her box

come, have a clue
the day is long   there
is light now on
the hills to see
by

The Youngest Pod

Time   restive
lying there, quiescent

bringing the strangeness home

savor of that hesitation lasts

puzzlement not actually expressive of anything
a series of moves   practice for
later life

a rhythm setting in
      able   *bodied*
fluttering frequency
"brain dump"

now, to work on organizing the nervous system

inscribing

      cradled
transits'   smooth head lulling
      cloudy milk at the sides of the mouth

approach   the whimper

young lungs too young   the
split light of late morning nearly punctures
      given over to
minisculist

what one's *what* is

      rear facing

      snow recedes along the
greasy path winter
weakens

dots sprinkle across infant's face   now
all is parenthetical

a clone
a motion

the
lawn
smells of an alternate
universe

       all irony fodder...

plummet lines' not straight

       aviary sound of the first spring rain
pervades

sand yellow shirt arms
      dusk
        falls without
quieting

untraceable   alternately

the wonderment the
mobile face

But even once you can see the fruits

But even once you can see the fruits
fresh
solution husks the
refrain loses steam under
midnight glare

so coded

clean line of riders bends
proverbial red balloon
under skids
willing a child to sleep
rumors sort by number
antiquely

      ergo
offspring
      sounds off

exhibiting
            sheer
      aptitude interrupts
the casing is not supposed to strain

adherence to a thought
      between times a small plane flies
into the window, yet again this
rare sitting

their wave edits antics
      her
ear aches

House Poem No. 2

Terrain frames
        notion of landscape as divorced
from land
        veracity of colors
                in what sense missing?
in what sense "missing out"?
unbelievable form of those clouds

while at base
clotted logic recoils

it's more true of the initiate

a limpid sky blue

sarcophagal

beyond which the green back of the neighbors' shed
just shows through   a blend
of optimism and terror

languid accord

        time lapse right here on the desk
                breeze from the east   odd
narrativized

"protect yourself from identity theft"

scattershot
ill-defined   solarium

        curricular pinch
        as soon as early morning ends

boy sleeps   so lovely
that he sleeps

what do you recognize and what do you
do about it

an edge

if you believe nothing else believe this

pentacoastal

waver of the will
      picture of a picture   posits

still air six a.m.
wall whites' subtle difference
thick spine of a volume of black & white images
of a city
catches my eye

stellar
      worst fire season in fifty years
squads quit   pell mell

      flames came into the region quickly

a lip a face a sun a ray cascades
      in thinking over the results

strange shape of trees' remains
directly to the left
      cool damp overcast   intermittent
rain impacts plans

"I explore conjunctions' outer edge"

page luge

most of the birds frequently

every head an icon

capitulate

the palate's work to refine sound production

      blue lights' glow hovers

a fond kind of nearly willful dumb

that algorithm's anagram

styrofoam cups floating amidst the
ponds' muck appear
almost natural, from a distance

how pleasing
speech attack
        ultimate inflow

in those needs alone arise

summers' end slow

actually it's a disaster area could you come some
other   decade?

detrital

fumigant
part animal part fear

shadowed
afterlife   in a dream a cyclone

third party drizzle

to know to *really* know
ones' sinuses

Made in the USA
Las Vegas, NV
21 December 2021